T0143872

WALKING CONTEMPLATIONS

REFLECTIONS ON RAMBLING AND AMBLING

TRIGGER
The mental health & wellbeing publisher

This edition published in 2023 by Trigger Publishing
An imprint of Shaw Callaghan Ltd

UK Office
The Stanley Building
7 Pancras Square
Kings Cross
London N1C 4AG

US Office
On Point Executive Center, Inc
3030 N Rocky Point Drive W
Suite 150
Tampa, FL 33607
www.triggerhub.org

A CIP catalogue record for this book is available
upon request from the British Library
ISBN: 9781837963874
Ebook ISBN: 9781837963881

Cover design and typeset by stevewilliamscreative.com

Trigger Publishing encourages diversity and different viewpoints. However, all
views, thoughts and opinions expressed in this book are the author's own and are
not necessarily representative of us as an organization.

All material in this book is set out in good faith for general guidance and no liability
can be accepted for loss or expense incurred in following the information given.
In particular this book is not intended to replace expert medical or psychiatric
advice. It is intended for informational purposes only and for your own personal
use and guidance. It is not intended to act as a substitute for professional medical
advice. The author is not a medical practitioner nor a counsellor, and professional
advice should be sought if desired before embarking on any health-related programme.

CONTENTS

ON FLORA AND FAUNA

In every walk with Nature one receives far more than he seeks.

JOHN MUIR, naturalist

Not until I went out could I tell that it was softly and coldly raining. Everything more than two or three fields away was hidden. Cycling is inferior to walking in this weather, because in cycling chiefly ample views are to be seen, and the mist conceals them. You travel too quickly to notice many small things; you see nothing save the troops of elms on the verge of invisibility. But walking I saw every small thing one by one; not only the handsome gateway chestnut just fully dressed, and the pale green larch plantation where another chiff-chaff was singing, and the tall elm tipped by a linnet pausing and musing a few notes, but every primrose and celandine and dandelion on the banks, every silvered green leaf of honeysuckle up in the hedge, every patch of brightest moss, every luminous drop on a thorn tip. The world seemed a small place: as I went between a row of elms and a row of beeches occupied by rooks, I had a feeling that the road, that the world itself, was private, all theirs; and the state of the road under their nests confirmed me. I was going hither and thither to-day in the neighbourhood of my stopping place, instead of continuing my journey.

EDWARD THOMAS, In Pursuit of Spring, (1914)

I walk regularly for my soul and my body tags along.

SARAH BAN BREATHNACH, author

A first walk in any new country is one of the things which make life on this planet worth being grateful for.

CHARLES WILLIAM BEEBE, explorer and naturalist

Every day at dawn my father used to take us for the most romantic walks, telling us stories about the places as we went: up the steep hill to Cudham Church; or to look for orchids at Orchis Bank, or along a legendary smuggler's track, or to the Big Woods where Uncle William had been lost as a child. The sudden valleys, the red, red earth full of strangely shaped flints, the great lonely woods, the sense of remoteness, made it different from any other place we knew. We were only sixteen miles from London Bridge, and yet it was so quiet that if a cart came down our lane we all rushed to look over the orchard wall to see it go by.

GWEN RAVERAT, Period Piece, a Cambridge Childhood, (1952)

And did those feet in ancient time

Walk upon England's mountains green?

WILLIAM BLAKE, poet

I only went out for a walk and finally concluded to stay out till sundown, for going out, I found, was really going in.

JOHN MUIR, naturalist

PAUSE FOR A THOUGHT

I chanced to rise very early one particular morning this summer, and took a walk into the country to divert myself among the fields and meadows, while the green was new, and the flowers in their bloom. As at this season of the year every lane is a beautiful walk, and every hedge full of nosegays, I lost myself, with a great deal of pleasure, among several thickets and bushes that were filled with a great variety of birds, and an agreeable confusion of notes, which formed the pleasantest scene in the world to one who had passed a whole winter in noise and smoke. The freshness of the dews that lay upon everything about me, with the cool breath of the morning, which inspired the birds with so many delightful instincts, created in me the same kind of animal pleasure, and made my heart overflow with such secret emotions of joy and satisfaction as are not to be described or accounted for.

JOSEPH ADDISON, Essay (1672-1719)

Us sing and dance, make faces and give flower bouquets, trying to be loved. You ever notice that trees do to git attention we do, except walk?

ALICE WALKER, author

PAUSE FOR THOUGHT

Travel does not merely broaden the mind. It makes the mind. Our early explorations are the raw materials of our intelligence... Children need paths to explore, to take bearings on the earth in which they live, as a navigator takes the bearings on familiar landmarks. If we excavate the memories of childhood, we remember the paths first, things and people second – paths down the garden, the way to school, the way round the house, corridors through the bracken or long grass. Tracking the paths of animals was the first and most important element in the education of early man.

SUSANNAH CLAPP, With Chatwin: Portrait of a Writer, (1997)

Why, one day in the country Is worth a month in the town

CHRISTINA ROSSETTI, poet

AMBLING ASIDE

The jacana is a southern hemisphere bird that walks across lily pads in search of snacks. To even its weight out across as large a surface as possible to avoid sinking, its toes are up to 10cm long. These are the longest toes of any bird in proportion to its size.

The wood I walk in on this mild May day, with the young yellowbrown foliage of the oaks between me and the blue sky, the white starflowers and the blue-eyed speedwell and the ground ivy at my feet – what grove of tropic palms, what strange ferns or splendid broadpetalled blossoms, could ever thrill such deep and delicate fibres within me as this home scene? Those familiar flowers, these well-remembered bird-notes, this sky with its fitful brightness, these furrowed and grassy fields, each with a sort of personality given to it by the capricious hedgerows – such things as these are the mother tongue of our imagination, the language that is laden with all the subtle inextricable associations the fleeting hours of our childhood left behind them.

GEORGE ELIOT, The Mill on the Floss, (1860)

The true charm of pedestrianism does not lie in the walking, or in the scenery, but in the talking. The walking is good to time the movement of the tongue by, and to keep the blood and the brain stirred up and active; the scenery and the woodsy smells are good to bear in upon a man an unconscious and unobtrusive charm and solace to eye and soul and sense; but the supreme pleasure comes from the talk.

MARK TWAIN, author

Walking connects you to the land, it sews a seam between you and it that is very hard to unstitch.

KELLY WINTERS, author

WALKING DREAM

**Interpretation by dream specialist
GUSTAVUS MILLER, 1901**

RAMBLE

To dream that you are rambling through the country denotes that you will be oppressed with sadness and separation from friends, but your worldly surroundings will be all that one could desire. For a young woman, this dream promises a comfortable home, but early bereavement.

ON JOURNEYS

Who is the third who walks always beside you?
When I count, there are only you and I together
But when I look ahead up the white road
There is always another one walking beside you
Gliding wrapt in a brown mantle, hooded
I do not know whether a man or a woman
– But who is that on the other side of you?

TS ELIOT, The Wasteland

One must always have one's boots

on and be ready to go

MICHEL DE MONTAIGNE, essayist

PAUSE FOR THOUGHT

I cannot see the wit of walking and talking at the same time. When I am in the country, I wish to vegetate like the country. I am not for criticising hedge-rows and black cattle. I go out of town in order to forget the town and all that is in it. There are those who for this purpose go to watering-places, and carry the metropolis with them. I like more elbow-room, and fewer incumbrances. I like solitude, when I give myself up to it, for the sake of solitude.

WILLIAM HAZLITT, On Going a Journe, (1822)

AMBLING ASIDE

THE WANDERING MINSTRELS

The family made famous by the 1965 Hollywood musical starring Julie Andrews was based on a true story. Captain Von Trapp did indeed marry a former nun who joined the family of seven children. They had three further children of their own and the final family of 12 formed the Von Trapp family singers. However, once Nazi Germany annexed Austria in 1938 they decided to flee their native country.

The Hollywood movie depicted the family fleeing the Nazis after a concert, walking over the Alps to freedom in Switzerland. In real life the family crossed the Alps to Italy. Once they had escaped the Third Reich on foot, they travelled to the US and settled in Stowe, Vermont where they continued to sing as a family to earn money.

Part of the pleasure of any kind of walking for me is the very idea of going somewhere – by foot.

RUTH RUDNER, author

On Tuesday I received a note from Jack Toledano asking me to meet him today at the Star and Garter in Putney at the usual time. I am used to these notes. Jack does not need to specify the time. If I cannot make it he goes for a walk himself, but I always try to be there because there is nothing better than going for a walk with Jack Toledano. London is a walker's paradise, he says, but you have to know where to go. Paris is for the flaneur, he says, but London is for the walker. The only way to think, he says, is at a desk, the only way to talk is on a walk.

GABRIEL JOSIPOVICI, author

A wanderer is man from birth

MATTHEW ARNOLD, poet

AMBLING ASIDE

The first verified walk around the world was by David Kunst (b 1939) who left his hometown of Waseca, Minnesota, USA heading east on 20th June 1970 and arrived back in Waseca from the west on 5th October, 1974. His walk took him through America, Europe, Asia and Australia. Kunst walked 14,450 miles, crossing four continents and thirteen countries, wearing out twenty-one pairs of shoes and walking more than twenty million steps.

'A journey of a thousand miles begins with a single step'

ANONYMOUS

I spent (the) day roaming through the valley. I stood beside the sources of the Arveiron, which take their rise in a glacier, that with slow pace is advancing down from the summit of the hills, to barricade the valley.

The abrupt sides of vast mountains were before me; the icy wall of the glacier overhung me; a few shattered pines were scattered around; and the solemn silence of this glorious presence-chamber of imperial Nature was broken only by the brawling waves, or the fall of some vast fragment, the thunder sound of the avalanche, or the cracking reverberating along the mountains of the accumulated ice, which, through the silent working of immutable laws, was ever and anon rent and torn, as if it had been but a plaything in their hands. These sublime and magnificent scenes afforded me the greatest consolation that I was capable of receiving. They elevated me from all littleness of feeling; and although they did not remove my grief, they subdued and tranquillised it. They congregated round me; the unstained snowy mountain-top, the glittering pinnacle, the pine woods, and ragged bare ravine; the eagle, soaring amidst the clouds – they all gathered round me, and bade me be at peace.

MARY SHELLEY, Frankenstein, (1823)

I may not have gone where I intended to go, but I think I have ended up where I intended to be.

DOUGLAS ADAMS, author

AMBLING ASIDE

Don Betty has been walking across suspension bridges for twenty-five years, his unusual pastime having taken him to bridges all over the world. In 1995, he was entered into the Guinness Book of World Records as the person who has walked across more suspension bridges than anyone else in the world.

Betty's obsession began in 1971, when he traversed a rope swing bridge suspended 240 feet across a canyon in British Columbia. Since then, he has crossed twenty-two of the twenty-five longest bridges in North America and twenty-two of the top twenty-five in the world. He has no plans to give up his hobby, despite recently having had an artificial leg fitted and undergoing open heart surgery – these hindrances have merely made taking photos of bridges more difficult. Betty's future plans include tackling bridges in Japan, Hong Kong, Denmark, Sweden and France.

Slow down and enjoy life. It's not only the scenery you miss by going too fast – you also miss the sense of where you are going and why.

EDDIE CANTOR, comedian and singer

I feared I might have got rusty, but all was well and my kit seemed in as good repair as the first day in Holland. The ammunition boots from Millets in the Strand, crunching along on their only slightly blunted hobnails, were still good for unlimited miles. The old breeches were soft with much wear and cleaning, and every stitch was intact; only the grey puttees had suffered minor damage, but nothing showed when I had snipped off the ragged edges where snow and rain had frayed them. A grey shirt with the sleeves rolled up completed this marching gear. I blessed my stars that my first rucksack, with its complex framework and straps, heavy water-proof sleeping-bag and White Knight superfluity of gear had been stolen in Munich; the one my Baltic Russian friends had bestowed was smaller but held all I needed; to wit: a pair of dark flannel bags and another light canvas pair; a thick, decent-looking tweed jacket; several shirts; two ties, gym-shoes, lots of socks and jerseys, pyjamas, the length of coloured braid Angela had given me; a dozen new handkerchiefs and a sponge-bag, a compass, a jack-knife, two candles, matches, a pipe – falling into disuse – tobacco, cigarettes and – a new accomplishment – papers for rolling them, and a flask-filled in turn, as the countries changed, with whisky, Bols, schnapps, barack, tzuica, slivovitz, arak and tziporo. In one of the side pockets there was a

five-shilling Ingersoll watch that kept perfect time when I remembered to take it out and wind it up.

The only awkward item was the soldier's greatcoat; I hadn't worn it for months, but felt reluctant to get rid of it. I still had the Hungarian walking-stick, intricately carved as a mediaeval crosier, the second replacement for the original ninepenny ashplant from the tobacconist's off Sloane Square. Apart from sketch-book, pencils and disintegrating maps, there was my notebook-journal and my passport. (Dog-eared and faded, these sole survivors are both within reach at this moment.) There was Hungarian and Rumanian Self-Taught (little progress in the one, hesitant first steps in the other); I was re-reading Antic Hay; and there was Schlegel & Tieck's Hamlet, Prinz von Danemark, bought in Cologne; also, given by the same kind hand as the rucksack, and carefully wrapped up, the beautiful little seventeenth-century duodecimo Horace from Amsterdam. It was bound in stiff, grass-green leather; the text had long s's; mezzotint vignettes of Tibur, Lucretilis and Bandusian spring, a scarlet silk marker, the giver's bookplate and a skeleton-leaf from his Estonian woods.

It would have been hard to set off much later than the cock crew that morning as the bird itself was flapping its wings on a barrel ten yards away, so I sloshed some water on my face and set off. It was going to be a sizzling day.

PATRICK LEIGH FERMOR, Between the Woods and the Water, (1986)

AMBLING ASIDE

GREAT SCOTT – GREATER COLLEAGUES?

The story of Captain Robert Falcon Scott's final walk in 1912 is well known. Having been beaten to the South pole by Norwegian rival Roald Amundsen (who had the cheek to be dragged there by teams of dogs, unlike the stiff-upper-lipped Scott, who insisted on walking every step of the way), he and his four men turned for home. Petty Officer Edgar Evans died on the way back, as did Captain Oates, who famously walked out of the tent one night – his birthday – announcing that he 'was just going outside, and may be some time'. Scott, Lt 'Birdie' Bowers and Dr Edward Wilson trudged on, dying about a dozen miles short of One Ton Depot, where food and fuel awaited them.

Scott's walk may be the most celebrated, but the overall expedition involved several other extraordinary feats on

foot, which are less well-known perhaps because they were more successful. After all, the English have always loved heroic failures.

- Many men set off in Scott's party to support the push for the pole, turning back in small groups at various stages of the route. Eventually the final three – the last men to see Scott's polar party alive – turned back. They were Lt "Teddy" Evans, PO Tom Crean, and PO William Lashly. On the way back to base camp, Lt Evans fell badly ill with scurvy. He could no longer walk. Crean and Lashly dragged him for several miles on the sledge, but he had become a burden. They pitched a tent, and while Lashly stayed with the invalid, Crean set off on the final thirty-five miles to get help. He wandered through a raging blizzard accompanied by nothing but two chocolate bars and three biscuits. He made it, and the rescue party saved both Evans and Lashly. Upon his arrival at base camp, Crean

was given a tot of brandy and some porridge, and promptly threw up. 'That's the first time in my life that ever it happened, and it was the brandy that did it,' said the rugged County Kerry man, who was to open a pub upon his return to Ireland.

• A few months before the polar push, three members of Scott's party set off on a scientific expedition to discover how emperor penguin eggs survived the harsh Antarctic weather. The three – Bowers, Wilson and Apsley Cherry-Garrard – hauled their sledge for sixty miles in freezing temperatures, lost their tent and lay huddled in sleeping bags for two days, sleepwalked in their own tracks, and finally made it back to camp with a cargo of eggs. Cherry-Garrard wrote up the tale a few years later as *The Worst Journey in the World*. 'If you march your Winter Journeys you will have your reward,' he wrote, 'so long as all you want is a penguin's egg'.

Many people will walk in and out of your life but only true friends will leave footprints in your heart

ELEANOR ROOSEVELT, stateswoman

One bright day in the last week of February, I was walking in the park, enjoying the threefold luxury of solitude, a book, and pleasant weather; for Miss Matilda had set out on her daily ride, and Miss Murray was gone in the carriage with her mamma to pay some morning calls. But it struck me that I ought to leave these selfish pleasures, and the park with its glorious canopy of bright blue sky, the west wind sounding through its yet leafless branches, the snowwreaths still lingering in its hollows, but melting fast beneath the sun, and the graceful deer browsing on its moist herbage already assuming the freshness and verdure of spring – and go to the cottage of one Nancy Brown.

ANNE BRONTE, Agnes Grey, (1847)

Man is not man sitting down: he is man on the move.

STEPHEN GRAHAM, journalist

AMBLING ASIDE

Emma Gatewood lived for most of her life on a farm, where she raised eleven children and four grandchildren, worked her fields, and planted flower and vegetable gardens. Her life changed at age seventy-one , when, after seeing a National Geographic article about the Appalachian Trail and discovering that no woman had ever hiked the entire length, Grandma Gatewood began her adventure. Her first attempt ended soon after she had started when she broke her spectacles and was forced to return home. In 1958, however, she successfully hiked the complete length of the trail from Maine to Georgia, only to repeat her achievement in 1960 and again in 1963. Grandma never brought with her the expensive paraphernalia so beloved of the modern hiker. She would always travel light, merely carrying a blanket, plastic sheet, cup, first aid kit, raincoat, and a change of clothes. Instead of walking boots, she chose an old

pair of tennis shoes. And there were no freeze-dried meals for her. Her meals consisted of dried beef, cheese and nuts, accompanied by any food that she might find along the path. Fans have ensured that her achievement is remembered by naming part of the Appalachian after her.

I had better admit right away that walking

can in the end become an addiction...

even in this final stage it remains a

delectable madness, very good for sanity,

and I recommend it with passion.

COLIN FLETCHER, author

WALKING DREAM

**Interpretation by dream specialist
GUSTAVUS MILLER, 1901**

WALKING

To dream of walking through rough briar-entangled paths denotes that you will be much distressed over your business complications, and disagreeable misunderstandings will produce coldness and indifference. To walk in pleasant places means you will be the possessor of fortune and favour. To walk in the night brings misadventure and unavailing struggle for contentment. For a young woman to find herself walking rapidly in her dreams denotes that she will inherit some property, and will possess a much desired object.

ON PATHWAYS

They shut the road through the woods
Seventy years ago.
Weather and rain have undone it again,
And now you would never know
There was once a path through the woods
Before they planted the trees,
It is underneath the coppice and the heath,
And the thin anemones.
Only the keeper sees
That, where the ring-dove broods,
And the badgers roll at ease,
There was once a road through the woods.
Yet, if you enter the woods
Of a summer evening late,
When the night-air cools on the trout-ring'd pools
Where the otter whistles his mate,
(They fear not men in the woods
Because they see so few)
You will hear the beat of a horse's feet
And the swish of a skirt in the dew,
Steadily cantering through
The misty solitudes,

As though they perfectly knew

The old lost road through the woods...

But there is no road through the woods.

RUDYARD KIPLING, The Way through the Woods

A vigorous five-mile walk will do more good for an unhappy but otherwise healthy adult than all the medicine and psychology in the world

PAUL DUDLEY WHITE, cardiologist

He and my father would often go for walks along the Warsaw Highway which cut across the countryside not far from our house. Sometimes I accompanied them. Scriabin liked to take a run and then to go on skipping along the road like a stone skimming the water, as if at any moment he might leave the ground and glide on air. In general, he had trained himself in various kinds of sublime lightness and unburdened movement verging on flight. Among such expressions of his character were his well-bred charm and his worldly manner of putting on a splendid air and avoiding serious subjects in society.

BORIS PASTERNAK, An Essay in Autobiography, (1959)

If you would grow great and stately, you must try to walk sedately.

ROBERT LOUIS STEVENSON, author

AMBLING ASIDE

IN THE FOOTSTEPS OF BUDDHA

One of the many interesting aspects of Buddhism is the tradition of Buddha footprints. Footprints are just one sign of the presence of the Buddha – the others being the bodhi tree, an umbrella, a throne, and the dharma, chakra or wheel of the Law.

Tradition holds that the Buddha (Gotama), or an incarnation known as 'the future Buddha' (Maitreya) left these behind to guide us to enlightenment.

When found in nature, these relics are subjected to extreme scrutiny to ensure they have all the right signs, then they become places of worship.

Footprints of the Buddha exist in Afghanistan, Bhutan, Cambodia, China, India, Japan, Korea, Laos, Malaysia, the Maldives, Pakistan, Singapore, Sri Lanka, Thailand

and Burma. The first footprints appeared during the appatima period that started in the earliest period of Buddhism and which remained strong until the fourth century.

Me thinks that the moment my legs begin to move, my thoughts begin to flow.

HENRY DAVID THOREAU, essayist

In the fifties and sixties, travelling on foot ceased to be a social degradation. The walking-tour became popular. It was not then called hiking, and it never should have been. Hiking suggests a strenuous covering of ground; what they did in the middle of century was the more leisurely stroll. Some of those foot travellers left accounts of their tours, and they make pleasant, quiet reading in these times. The few accounts one has seen of hiking have something of a crowd and clamour about them; they do not convey the spirit of the true walking-tour, the spirit of solitude and calm which arises from the books of the time.

THOMAS BURKE, Travel in England, (1942)

Thoughts come clearly while one walks.

THOMAS MANN, author

AMBLING ASIDE

Camina de Santiago is an 800km route from southern France across Northern Spain, to Santiago de Compostela. The site was originally founded by St James, whose body was also buried here after he was killed in Palestine. His remains were discovered in the ninth century and the area became a centre of pilgrimage for Christians, thousands of whom still walk there today.

Walking, ideally, is a state in which the mind, the body, and the world are aligned, as though they were three characters finally in conversation together, three notes suddenly making a chord.

REBECCA SOLNIT, author

PAUSE FOR THOUGHT

Once trodden by human feet, a natural path becomes a work of man, each traveller marking the way for the next, sometimes departing from the most direct or obvious route to avoid a muddy patch, or to keep out of sight of possible enemies. Feet follow footsteps, and so a road is trodden into history.

J.R.L. ANDERSON AND FAY GODWIN, The Oldest Road: An Exploration of the Ridgeway, (1975)

I will clamber through the clouds and exist

JOHN KEATS, poet

AMBLING ASIDE

For ancient Greeks the oracle at the temple of Apollo at Delphi became famous for answering devotees' questions. It was even consulted for advice on affairs of states. Delphi was known as the navel of the world – a spiritual, and geographic centre where thousands came to seek help. In fact so many journeyed to Delphi that oracles, which had been given out once a year, were increased to once a month. Travellers came to this shrine on Mount Parnassus from Greece, Egypt and Asia Minor.

'The walker's companions are the stones in his boot, the rain in his face, the unreadable map...

...but a wide-open space'

ANONYMOUS

He was a peasant, but he was a rambler also... He loved winter as he did the mountains, and probably the sea in the same way, though the Muse did claim to have seen him 'seek the sounding shore, delighted with the dashing roar'. She said, too, that she had seen him struck by 'Nature's visage hoar' under the north wind, and he has told us himself that 'There is scarcely any earthly object gives me more – I don't know if I should call it pleasure, but something which exalts me, something which enraptures me – than to walk in the sheltered side of a wood or high plantation, in a cloudy winter day, and hear a stormy wind howling among the trees and raving o'er the plain.'

EDWARD THOMAS, On Robert Burns: A Literary Pilgrim in England, (1917)

I dream of hiking into my old age. I want to be able even then to pack my load and take off slowly but steadily along the trail.

MARILYN DOAN, author

AMBLING ASIDE

Glastonbury is a worldwide recognised site of pilgrimage, not only for Christian pilgrims but pilgrims of every denomination and belief. For Christians Glastonbury is the revered site of the first Christian church built in the British Isles by Joseph of Arimathea. For others it is the resting place of Arthur and the home of the quest for the Grail and all the legends that surround it.

The growing interest in sacred places has led to a modern awakening in the value of pilgrimage. In every age there have been pilgrims travelling to the sacred sites and places of the world as an act of spiritual devotion to their particular creed.

I was the only kid who anybody I knew has ever seen actually walk into a lamppost with his eyes wide open. Everybody assumed that there must be something going on inside, because there sure as hell wasn't anything going on on the outside!

DOUGLAS ADAMS, author

Unable to resist the sun, so I caught the ten train and walked across the meadow (buttercups, forget-me-nots, ragged robins) to the Dipper stream and the ivy bridge. Read ardently in Geology till twelve. Then took off my boots and socks, and waded underneath the right arch of the bridge in deep water, and eventually sat on a dry stone at the top of the masonry just where the water drops into the green salmon pool in a solid bar. Next I wandered upstream to a big slab of rock tilted at a comfortable angle. I lay flat on this with my nether extremities in water up to my knees. The sun bathed my face and dragon flies chased up and down intent on murder. But I cared not a tinker's Demetrius about Nature red in tooth and claw. I was quite satisfied with Nature under a June sun in the cool atmosphere of a Dipper stream. I lay on the slab completely relaxed, and the cool water ran strongly between my toes. Surely I was never again going to be miserable. The voices of children playing in the wood made me extra happy. For these were fairy voices ringing through enchanted woods.

W.N.P. BARBELLION, The Journal of a Disappointed Man, (1919)

Walk and be happy, walk and be healthy. The best way to lengthen out our days is to walk steadily and with a purpose.

CHARLES DICKENS, author

AMBLING ASIDE

Mount Kailash is a pilgrimage site in Tibet revered by Hindus, Buddhist, Jains and Bonpos. A single circuit of the 32 km route round the base will – according to some – ease the sins of a lifetime. The pilgrimage continued for thousands of years until the Chinese invasion of Tibet. Now only 200 pilgrims are allowed to enter the site from India. To join them you would have to enter a lucky draw run by the Indian government, and undergo two days of physical tests in a Delhi hospital to make sure you are fit enough. After all, the site is 22,028 feet high.

It is good to collect things; it is better to take walks.

ANATOLE FRANCE, poet and author

WALKING DREAM

**Interpretation by dream specialist
GUSTAVUS MILLER, 1901**

WALKING STICK

To see a walking stick in a dream foretells that you will enter into contracts without proper deliberation, and will consequently suffer reverses. If you use one in walking, you will be dependent upon the advice of others. To admire handsome ones, you will entrust your interests to others, but they will be faithful.

ON WALKING LORE

Jog on, jog on, the footpath way
And merrily hent the stile-a:
A merry heart goes all the day,
Your sad tires in a mile-a.

WILLIAM SHAKESPEARE, A Winter's Tale

Never ride when you can walk.

BILL GALE, author

At three o'clock Cummings and Gowing called for a good long walk over Hampstead and Finchley, and brought with them a friend named Stillbrook. We walked and chatted together, except Stillbrook, who was always a few yards behind us staring at the ground and cutting at the grass with his stick.

As it was getting on for five, we four held a consultation, and Gowing suggested that we should make for The Cow and Hedge and get some tea. Stillbrook said a brandy and soda was good enough for him. I reminded them that all public houses were closed till six o'clock.

Stillbrook said, 'That's alright – bona-fide travellers.'

We arrived; and as I was trying to pass, the man in charge of the gate said: 'Where from?' I replied: 'Holloway'. He immediately put up his arm, and declined to let me pass. I turned back for a moment, when I saw Stillbrook, closely followed by Cummings and Gowing, make for the entrance. I watched them, and thought I would have a good laugh at their expense. I heard the porter say: 'Where from?' When, to my surprise, in fact disgust, Stillbrook replied: 'Blackheath,' and the three were immediately admitted.

Gowing called to me across the gate, and said: 'We shan't be a minute.' I waited for them the best part of an hour.

GEORGE AND WEEDON GROSSMITH, The Diary of a Nobody, (1892)

Everywhere is within walking distance if you have the time.

STEVEN WRIGHT, comedian

AMBLING ASIDE

Weather Lore

"Rain before seven; fine before eleven"

Generally, a given area is unlikely to experience rain from a low-pressure system for long periods, and rainfall that starts the previous evening will probably cease before noon.

Walking is easiest, you don't need a lot of apparatus. Just shoe leather and good feet.

PAUL DUDLEY WHITE, cardiologist

Tips on taking a perambulation, taken from a 19th century journal:

Gentlemen walking with a lady will give her the inner path, unless the outer part of the walk is safer. This move will be made without remark, and the lady will assume whenever the gentleman changes his position that there is a sufficient reason for moving from one side to the other.

A lady in the street or park may not be saluted by a gentleman, unless he has first received a slight bow from the lady. He may then raise his hat with the hand farthest from the lady, bow respectfully and pass on, not stopping to speak under any circumstance, unless the lady pauses in her promenade.

When gentlemen unaccompanied by ladies meet, each will raise his hat very slightly, if they are on such terms as to warrant recognition. They will bow only if the person saluted commands special respect, by reason of advanced years, social rank, or attainments, or having taken holy orders. In every such case a gentleman will raise the hat with the hand farthest from the person saluted, but the head need not be completely uncovered.

When a gentleman is escorting a lady in any public place, it is his duty to insist on carrying any article she may have in her hand,

except her parasol when it is being used as a sunshade.

When gentlemen pause to speak to each other on the street, they will, as a matter of course, shake hands and bow, lifting the hat with the left hand at the moment of their clasping the right.

Gentlemen will never smoke when walking with a lady, as although there is no intentional disrespect in smoking, the act may suggest to other persons a lesser regard for the lady.

Gentlemen walking together may use any pace not actually violent or ungraceful; but when accompanying ladies, aged persons, or the weak, they will accommodate themselves to their companions.

Gentlemen will not swing their arms, nor sway their bodies in an ungainly fashion when walking.

Ladies are never guilty of any such ungraceful action, and need no counsel in that respect.

Ladies sometimes, though very rarely, walk too quickly on the street. That should be avoided; a message by telephone will generally obviate the necessity for speed at the expense of grace.

Ladies walking on the street are not expected to recognise gentlemen or friends on the other side of the road. To do so would necessitate habits of observation inconsistent with ladylike repose.

Of all exercises, walking is the best.

THOMAS JEFFERSON, former US president

AMBLING ASIDE

"If the moon rises haloed round; soon you'll tread on deluged ground"

A blurred or watery moon or a solar halo is caused by the ice crystals in altostratus or cirrostratus clouds – the clouds are a sure sign of a rainbelt approaching, probably within five to eight hours

Before supper walk a little; after supper do the same.

DESIDERIUS ERASMUS ROTERODAMUS, humanist and theologian

Now, to be properly enjoyed, a walking tour should be gone upon alone. If you go in company, or even in pairs, it is no longer a walking tour in anything but name; it is something else and more in the nature of a picnic. A walking tour should be gone upon alone, because freedom is of the essence; because you should be able to stop and go on, and follow this way or that, as the freak takes you; and because you must have your own pace, and neither trot alongside a champion walker, nor mince in time with a girl.

ROBERT LOUIS STEVENSON, Walking Tour, (1881)

The body's habituation to walking as normal stems from the good old days. It was the bourgeois form of locomotion: physical demythologization, free of the spell of hieratic pacing, roofless wandering, breathless flight. Human dignity insisted on the right to walk, a rhythm not extorted from the body by command or terror. The walk, the stroll, were private ways of passing time, the heritage of the feudal promenade in the nineteenth century.

THEODOR W ADORNO, philosopher

AMBLING ASIDE

Red sky at night, shepherd's delight
Red sky in the morning, shepherd's warning.

This famous saying may well have Biblical origins. In Matthew 16:2–3, Christ says:

'When it is evening, ye say, it will be fair weather: for the sky is red. And in the morning, it will be foul weather today: for the sky is red and lowering.'

There is truth in the saying. As any good shepherd could tell you, a pale rosy evening sky with little cloud is a sign of fair weather, haze particles causing the light to bend and creating the pinkish glow. About seven out of ten red sunsets herald good weather the following day. However, a deep red glow under thick cloud, often visible at sunset or at dawn, is a good indication of rain.

The rich colour is caused by light bending through water droplets in the atmosphere.

The sole criterion is to walk with the senses, with hands that feel, ears that hear, and eyes that see.

ROBERT BROWNE, author

Two men were travelling together, when a bear suddenly met them on their path. One of them climbed up quickly into a tree and concealed himself in the branches. The other, seeing that he must be attacked, fell flat on the ground, and when the bear came up and felt him with his snout, and smelt him all over, he held his breath, and feigned the appearance of death as much as he could. The bear soon left him, for it is said he will not touch a dead body. When he was quite gone, the other traveller descended from the tree, and jocularly inquired of his friend what it was the bear had whispered in his ear. 'He gave me this advice,' his companion replied. 'Never travel with a friend who deserts you at the approach of danger.'

AESOP, Fables, (600 BCE)

You have to stay in shape. My grandmother, she started walking five miles a day when she was sixty. She's ninety-seven today and we don't know where the hell she is.

ELLEN DEGENERES, comedian

AMBLING ASIDE

ETYMOLOGY

Ramble From the Middle Dutch, *rammelen*: to wander about in sexual excitement (usually applied to night wanderings of cats); and rammen, to copulate.

Walk From the Old English *wealcan*: to roll, toss or wander.

Amble From the Latin *ambulare*: to walk.

Stroll Probably from the German *strolch*: a vagabond.

March From the French *marcher*: to walk.

Blister From the Old French *blestre*: a swelling or pimple.

Rucksack From the German *rucken*: back, and Greek sakkos, sack.

Trail From the Latin *tragul*: a dragnet.

Thermos From the Greek *thermo*: hot

Walking is man's best medicine.

HIPPOCRATES, Ancient Greek physician

How much you get from walking will depend, in the last resort, upon yourself, rather than the country. One mind will get more out of a few fields than another will from a range of mountains. It is a matter of developing a breadth of interests. For myself, I love all historical things, and, though knowing not the first elements of architecture, derive pleasure from castles, cathedrals, inns and cottages. For the minutiae of Nature I have no aptitude. I am continually and infuriatingly baffled by my inability to name the little hedges, the birds, and other retiring beauties of the country. The ideal walker would, I suppose, have geology and all other -ologies at his fingertips. He would be steeped in history and literary associations. He would be able to analyse a cathedral into its constituent parts and tag each with a date and style. He would talk knowledgeably to the locals about crops and crafts and industries. Such a man (supposing his head did not burst) would cover about one mile in a summer's day. I prefer to air my ignorance on the hills and walk twenty, noticing what I can. But certainly a little knowledge of all or any of these things, far from being dangerous, adds immensely to one's pleasure.

GEOFFREY TREASE, Walking in England, (1936)

Walk a day, live a week.

OLD FRENCH PROVERB

AMBLING ASIDE

THE RULES OF WALKABOUT

The Australian Aboriginal concept of "walkabout" promotes self-discovery and challenge as important parts of our life's passage. Yet, traditionally, walkabouts are completed in pairs, discussing an issue or dilemma with a partner. There are certain accepted rules acknowledged by two people who go walkabout together.

1. The conversation is confidential, and may not be repeated to anyone else. Similarly, neither partner may later approach the other for an update on the conversation, unless previously agreed.

2. Each partner has the same amount of time to discuss their issues.

3. The pace should never be hurried. The third occasional partner on a walkabout is silence.

I have two doctor:, my left leg and my right.

GEORGE M TREVELYAN, historian

WALKING DREAMS

Interpretation by dream specialist
GUSTAVUS MILLER, 1901

<u>CLIMBING</u>

To dream of climbing up a hill or mountain and reaching the top, you will overcome the most formidable obstacles between you and a prosperous future; but if you should fail to reach the top, your dearest plans will suffer being wrecked.

TriggerHub.org is one of the most elite and scientifically proven forms of mental health intervention

Trigger Publishing is the leading independent mental health and wellbeing publisher in the UK and US. Clinical and scientific research conducted by assistant professor Dr Kristin Kosyluk and her highly acclaimed team in the Department of Mental Health Law & Policy at the University of South Florida (USF), as well as complementary research by her peers across the US, has independently verified the power of lived experience as a core component in achieving mental health prosperity. Specifically, the lived experiences contained within our bibliotherapeutic books are intrinsic elements in reducing stigma, making those with poor mental health feel less alone, providing the privacy they need to heal, ensuring they know the essential steps to kick-start their own journeys to recovery, and providing hope and inspiration when they need it most.

Delivered through TriggerHub, our unique online portal and accompanying smartphone app, we make our library of bibliotherapeutic titles and other vital resources accessible to individuals and organizations anywhere, at any time and with complete privacy, a crucial element of recovery. As such, TriggerHub is the primary recommendation across the UK and US for the delivery of lived experiences.

At Trigger Publishing and TriggerHub, we proudly lead the way in making the unseen become seen. We are dedicated to humanizing mental health, breaking stigma and challenging outdated societal values to create real action and impact. Find out more about our world-leading work with lived experience and bibliotherapy via triggerhub.org, or by joining us on:

𝕏 @triggerhub_

⬤ @triggerhub.org

⬤ @triggerhub_

Printed in the USA
CPSIA information can be obtained
at www.ICGtesting.com
JSHW012051140824
68134JS00035B/3377

9 781837 963874